Loons

GEORGE K. PECK

SMART APPLE MEDIA

Published by

Smart Apple Media

123 South Broad Street

Mankato, Minnesota 56001

☙

Copyright © 1998 Smart Apple Media.

International copyrights reserved in all countries.

No part of this book may be reproduced in any form without

written permission from the publisher.

Printed in the United States of America.

Photos by George K. Peck,

Mark Peck,

Bill Ivy

Editorial assistance by Barbara Ciletti

Library of Congress Cataloging-in-Publication Data

Peck, George K.

Loons / written by George Peck.

p. cm.

Includes index.

Summary: Describes the physical characteristics, behaviors, and habitats

of various species of the oldest existing family of birds, the loons.

ISBN 1-887068-10-4

1. Loons—Juvenile literature.   2. Common loons—Juvenile literature.

I. Title.

QL696.G33P435   1998   96-18156

598.4'42—dc20   CIP

AC

First Edition   5 4 3 2 1

C O N T E N T S

Sixty-five million years ago, while dinosaurs still roamed the earth, a long-bodied bird with a pointed-toothed bill and webbed feet swam through an ancient sea.

We do not know the color of that ancient bird's feathers, or the sound of its cry, but early fossils give us its shape and its size.

It looked similar to a giant loon.

Loons are the oldest family of birds on earth. No other living bird family has survived for so long with so few changes. Early North American Indians such as the Algonquin, Ojibwa, and Cree, believed that loons had magical powers. Today the loon continues to fascinate us.

When you see a loon, it is as if you are seeing into the past.

There are five species of loons. All are known for their striking appearance and mournful voices: the Red-throated Loon, the Arctic Loon, the Pacific Loon, the Yellow-billed Loon, and the Common Loon. All five species are found in North America.

The Red-throated Loon is the most widely distributed species, spending its summers in the treeless areas of northern Canada, Alaska, Greenland, and Eurasia. In the winter, the Red-throated Loon can be found along the east and west coasts of North America, and occasionally on the Great Lakes.

The Pacific Loon and the Yellow-billed Loon spend their summers in northern Canada and Alaska, and winter along the west coast as far south as the Baja Peninsula. The Arctic Loon is found in Eurasia and western Alaska.

The Common Loon is seen on lakes all across Canada and the northern United States during the summer months. They are also found as far east as Scotland. In the winter, the Common Loon lives along the east and west coasts of North America as far south as Florida in the east, and Mexico in the west. A few Common Loons spend their winters on the Great Lakes.

Loons live in many different parts of the northern hemisphere, but always on or next to a lake, ocean, or river. You will never see a loon walking across a cornfield, or perched in a tree. Loons are built for a life on and in the water, and that is where they spend almost their entire lives. They even sleep while floating on the water!

Red-throated Loon sitting on nest.

Why do modern loons look like their ancient ancestors? Maybe it's because their bodies are perfectly designed for their watery habitat.

Their strong, webbed feet are set far back on the body, which helps propel them through the water. Their wings are long, narrow, and powerful. In the air, their rapid beat can propel the loon to speeds of up to 100 miles per hour (160 kph). When diving underwater, their wings are used for balance and turning. The loon's streamlined body moves easily through the water or through the air. Don't expect to see loons walking on land, though. Their legs are designed for swimming, not strolling.

Most flying birds have evolved lightweight bones with air sacs. Lighter bones make flying easier. But loons have somewhat heavy bones without air sacs, like their ancestors millions of years in the past. The loon's heavier skeleton may help it dive deeper in search of food, but it also makes takeoff difficult. Watching a loon fly from the surface of a lake is a little like watching a big airplane—it takes a long runway to get it into the air.

Loons are large birds, about the size of geese. The Common Loon is 28 to 36 inches long (71 to 91 cm), with a wingspread of 58 inches (147 cm) or nearly 5 feet across. It weighs 6 1/2 to 8 1/2 pounds (3 to 4 kg).

Like many waterbirds, loons have a preen gland near their tail. They use their beaks and wings to spread oil from this gland onto their feathers. The oil helps the feathers shed water, keeping the loon's body dry and warm.

The loon's neck and head feathers are velvety and soft, but its body feathers are thick, water-resistant, and hard to the touch. Beneath the body feathers is a layer of semi-plume feathers, and next to the skin is a layer of fine down. These inner layers of feathers hold air to insulate the bird's body and make it easier for the loon to float.

In the summer the Common Loon has a black head with a greenish, iridescent tint. Its wings and parts of its back are covered with a beautiful pattern of small white squares and spots, and its neck is wrapped by a necklace of short white stripes. The loon's breast and belly are pure white. It has a sharp, straight, black bill and ruby red eyes. Red eyes are a feature shared by all loons. Male and female loons look the same, but the female is slightly smaller.

In winter, the Common Loon is less colorful. Its head and back are brownish gray, with a white throat and belly, a gray beak, and dark eyes. All loon species have similar brownish-gray and white plumage during the winter.

The Yellow-billed Loon, the largest member of the family, looks like a longer and heavier version of the Common Loon, weighing as much as 14 pounds (6.3 kg). It can be identified by its upturned yellow- or ivory-colored bill.

The smallest loon is the Red-throated Loon. It is about 25 inches long (64 cm) and weighs only 3 to 4 pounds (1.5 to 2 kg). It has a gray head with white stripes on the back of the neck and a red patch on its throat.

Arctic and Pacific Loons are very difficult to tell apart. In summer plumage, they have gray heads, backs and wings decorated with a pattern of white squares, and an iridescent green or purple patch on their throats. They were once thought to be the same species.

Loons are skillful hunters. They dive deep beneath the surface, using their powerful webbed feet to propel their streamlined bodies, searching for fish. Loons depend on their eyes to spot their dinner. They hunt during the daylight and in clear water where they can see fish from a distance. Most loons prefer to hunt from 6 to 15 feet (1.8 to 4.5 m) below the surface, but they can dive much deeper. The Common Loon can dive as deep as 240 feet (73 m) and has been seen to swim underwater for a distance of 1,640 feet (500 m). Their dives usually last less than a minute, but a loon can hold its breath for more than five minutes.

Loons burn up a lot of energy and have big appetites. They eat small catfish, perch, and other freshwater fish during the summer. In winter they feed on ocean fish such as herring, cod, and sand eels. They are also willing to sample frogs, crabs, snails, crayfish, insects, and occasionally some plants. Perhaps one of the reasons the loon family has survived for millions of years is because they are able to eat lots of different foods. If there are no herring to be had, a squid will do!

Because of their large bodies and heavy bones, loons can't just jump into the air and fly away. Only the smaller Red-throated Loon can take off from land. Other loons need a running start on the water. A Common Loon might have to go the length of four football fields—flapping its wings and running on the surface of the water—before it gets going fast enough to take off!

Once in the air, loons are strong, swift flyers. Their narrow, pointed wings beat 250 times per minute. In the air, loons do not wheel and turn and circle like some other birds. Loons seem to know exactly where they are going. The loon flies straight and fast, with its head held low, its sharp beak leading the way, and its webbed feet trailing behind.

Twice each year, all loons migrate. In the spring, they fly north and inland to the lakes where they will breed. In the fall, they fly south, toward the sea, where the waters are warmer and there are plenty of fish.

In late summer or fall, Common Loons begin their migration south. Sometimes a loon will fly alone, or they may gather in small groups of up to 15 birds. Loons may fly more than 1 1/4 miles (2 km) above the earth. It takes a hard rain or dense fog to make a loon delay its migration flight.

In the spring, the loons begin their journey back to the freshwater lakes where they were born. Because loons can't eat or take off from a frozen lake, they time their migration to follow the breakup of the ice. Male loons are one of the first waterbirds to show up in the spring.

Migrating Common Loons in Ontario.

Loons mate for life (about 15 to 30 years) or for as long as either partner lives. During the winter, the male and female loons may go their separate ways. But every spring, they return to the same territory where they made their first nest.

A loon's territory might be a whole lake, or a bay on a larger lake or river. It must be deep enough for them to escape from enemies by diving. It must be big enough to allow takeoffs and landings. And it must have a good supply of fish. A deep lake with small islands is ideal.

The male loon arrives first in the spring. If another loon has invaded its territory, it will drive off the intruder by calling out, splashing the water with its wings, or attacking. When the female arrives a few weeks later, the courtship begins.

The pair of loons swim together, often side by side, with their bills pointed straight up. They may rush around in a circle on the surface of the lake, calling back and forth to each other. Sometimes they take to the air together, still calling and flying around in circles, until they decide to land on the water together, breast first, with a great splash. These noisy courtship displays often happen at night.

Loons use several different calls. During courtship, the male calls to the female with a sound called a "yodel," that goes up and down in pitch. A single loon approaching a group often hoots, with a soft, careful one-note call.

When a mother loon searches for one of her chicks she makes a long call known as a "wail," which may also be used to contact a mate.

The most commonly heard call is the "tremolo." It sounds like a crazy person laughing. The loon's wild laughter is the reason for the expression "crazy as a loon," but the loon is not crazy—it may be warning other loons of possible danger.

The loon is also known to add a display to its wild and lonely laugh, especially if intruders come close to the nest or the chicks. The loon rushes at the intruder, rising up out of the water with its head drawn back and its bill almost touching its breast. Meanwhile, its feet beat away at the water, creating a spray that surrounds the dancing body. After that, the loon may dive, rise to the surface, and repeat the whole noisy performance. Most visitors leave the scene in a hurry.

Loons mate on the shore and choose a nest site that may be very close to the one used the year before. Most loons nest on islands, where they are safe from large predators. They also build nests on muskrat houses and on the mainland shore. Nests are always very close to the water, so that the loons can dive underwater quickly if danger threatens. Sometimes nests are built up a few feet from the shore in shallow water. A good nesting site has a view of the surrounding area, as well as protection from wind and waves.

The male and the female work together, gathering materials and preparing the nest for their future family. Nests are usually hidden in tall rushes and grasses. The nest itself is about 1 1/2 feet across and is made of rushes, grass, mud, and small twigs. Once in a while a loon pair will not bother making a nest at all, and the female will lay her eggs in a hollow on the bare ground.

Loons raise only one brood of chicks each year. But if a nest is destroyed by weather or by predators, they will sometimes build a new nest and try again!

Usually the mother lays two eggs that are about the size of pears. The eggs are brown and covered with dark brown or black spots. Taking turns sitting on the eggs, the parents incubate them for about 29 days. Their body heat helps the eggs develop.

A built-up nest of the Red-throated Loon in Canada's Northwest Territories.

The baby loons hatch one at a time, one day apart. One day there is one chick, and the next day there are two. The babies are wet when they hatch, and covered with downy plumes within cases of fine tissue. As the newborn chicks move around, the tips of the cases split and fall apart, and the new feathers dry off. Black down covers everything but their breasts, which are a soft light gray. About three hours later, the chicks look like balls of black fluff. Their eyes are wide open. They're ready for their first swim.

As soon as both babies take to the water, the loon family abandons its nest. But they are far from homeless. The loons move to a "nursery" area—a shallow, protected bay that is out of the wind. It must have plenty of small fish, and lots of hiding places in case of danger.

Two days after hatching, baby loons can dive about 1 foot (.3 m) under the surface of the water. When they are tired from all the exercise, they ride on their parents' backs, resting and staying warm and safe. After 10 to 14 days they are diving often and can swim 20 to 30 yards (18 to 27 m) underwater.

Loon chicks grow very rapidly, so they need to eat a lot. During their first week, they eat as often as 73 times in one day. You may eat breakfast, lunch and dinner, and probably a snack after school. That's four meals. Just imagine what it would be like to eat 69 more meals a day. Baby loons are always hungry, but they don't know how to get food. They are fed small fish by their parents. When they are one week old, they learn to catch a few small minnows.

As the weeks go by, the family travels farther and farther away from the nursery and the parents continue to bring food to the babies, even though they can now eat by themselves. By eight weeks the adults forage more and more for themselves, forcing the chicks to search for their own food. The chicks have grown into fledglings, which means that they have almost all of their outer feathers, and their feet are almost as big as their parents' feet.

The fledglings are ready to fly when they are 10 to 12 weeks old. As with all birds, flying is instinctive. As soon as the young loons' wings are strong enough, they take to the air. Once the loons can fly and feed themselves, they are on their own.

The most dangerous times for a loon are while it is still in its egg or when it is very young. Foxes, raccoons, skunks, mink, and other predators seek out loon nests. Even some birds such as gulls, ravens, and crows have been known to raid loon nests and eat the eggs. Baby loons are sometimes attacked from underwater by large pike or snapping turtles.

Adult loons are fast and strong, and have little to fear from predators. Dangers to adult loons mostly come from human beings. Many loons are killed by oil spills, or are caught in fishing nets. Air pollution from automobiles and factories causes acid rain, which kills the fish in many of the loon's breeding lakes. The noise and waves caused by motorboats disturbs nesting loons, sometimes causing them to desert their eggs.

Human beings have lived on Earth for millions of years.

Loons have been here ten times longer. The loon family has survived ice ages, droughts, floods, and other natural disasters. Their adaptability has helped them survive tremendous changes to our planet's surface. While other species have disappeared or changed beyond recognition, loons have remained almost the same.

When we hear the wild laughter of a loon, we hear echos of the distant past. But does the call of the loon also echo into the future?

As long as loons are given the space and the privacy to breed, and as long as there are fish in our lakes and oceans, loons will survive. They will remain a part of our natural world. Your grandchildren will hear the call of the loon 100 years from now. And in another 65 million years, who knows? Maybe we will all be gone, only remembered by the loons.

I N D E X